WHAT WOULD
WINSTON
DO?

WHAT WOULD
WINSTON
DO?

DADS ASK THEIR QUESTIONS, WINSTON
PROVIDES THE ANSWERS

ED ENFIELD

SPHERE

First published in Great Britain in 2021 by Sphere

1 3 5 7 9 10 8 6 4 2

Copyright © Little, Brown Book Group 2021

The moral right of the author has been asserted.

All the people mentioned in this book, bar Winston Churchill, are fictional.
Any similarities to real people are entirely coincidental.

Churchill illustration: Natata/Shutterstock

A CIP catalogue record for this book is available from the British Library.

ISBN 978-0-7515-8050-1

Typeset in Bembo by M Rules
Printed and bound in Great Britain by Clays Ltd, Elcograf S.p.A.

Papers used by Sphere are from well-managed forests
and other responsible sources.

Sphere
An imprint of
Little, Brown Book Group
Carmelite House
50 Victoria Embankment
London EC4Y 0DZ

An Hachette UK Company
www.hachette.co.uk

www.littlebrown.co.uk

For Dad

Writing a book is an adventure.

WINSTON CHURCHILL

Contents

Introduction

Sir Winston Leonard Spencer-Churchill, Britain's prime minister for the greater part of the Second World War and again from 1951 to 1955, had many secrets. One was that in his spare time, usually in the wee hours of the morning when the country was asleep, he liked to play agony aunt to the fathers in his constituency and beyond. It is *not* a secret that Sir Winston was a man of many wise words and – having fathered five children with his wife, Clementine – he took pity on the dads, pops, pas, das, daddys and pappys throughout the land, making his considerable advice available to them through letters written on an Imperial typewriter.

In a recent excavation of the garden shed at Chartwell, Sir Winston's home from 1922 until his death in 1965, copies of these letters were unearthed. Given the great man's love for spreading his words far and wide, it seemed only fitting to collate them into a book – so that other fathers feeling their way through the trials and tribulations of fatherhood can benefit from their sage guidance. It has been the highlight and privilege of my career to shoulder this responsibility.*

Ed Enfield

---

* To clarify, very little of this paragraph is true, but wouldn't it be great if it was? The quotes in this book are all reported Winston Churchill words, applied to modern-day simulated parenting questions.

REGARDING YOUNG CHILDREN

Dear Winston,

We're trying to get our baby to self-soothe and it's proving tricky. Can you give us any advice?

George, 29, Dudley

Learn to get used to it. Eels get used to skinning.

Dear Winston,

My son keeps talking back to me and I'm
rubbish at telling him off for it. What
should I say to him when he does it?

Jack, 37, Southend-on-Sea

> If I valued
> the honourable
> gentleman's
> opinion I might
> get angry.

Dear Winston,

My children keep saying that they hate each other. What should I say to them?

Harry, 35, Norwich

I hate nobody except Hitler — and that is professional.

Dear Winston,

My son is six and he will not sit still.
What can I say to him to calm him
down?

Muhammad, 41,
Milton Keynes

The honourable
gentleman should
really not generate
more indignation than
he can conveniently
contain.

Dear Winston,

My daughter is eight and she's being so naughty at school that we've got to have a meeting with the headmaster about it. What should I say to her to get her to behave?

Vinay, 42, Hull

Headmasters have powers at their disposal with which prime ministers have never yet been invested.

Dear Winston,

My daughter is only seven and she's already asked me how her mum and I made her. I don't want to lie to her, but I don't want to tell her the truth either. What should I say?

Freddie, 40, Blackpool

I think 'No comment' is a splendid expression.

Dear Winston,

My son has just started to walk! He keeps falling over but he gets right back up again. Can I have a congratulatory message for him?

Ethan, 25, Reading

The greatest living master of falling without hurting himself.

Dear Winston,

My daughter's growing up so fast and I'm
finding it really sad. Any rousing words?

Arthur, 34, Luton

To improve
is to change;
to be perfect
is to change
often.

Dear Winston,

My baby hasn't slept through the night in two months. Help!

Oliver, 27, Portsmouth

Megalomania
is the only
form of
sanity.

Dear Winston,

My daughter's friend is addicted to gaming. What should I say to my daughter so she won't want to take it up quite so religiously?

Jacob, 28, Bolton

> I have never seen a human being who more perfectly represented the modern concept of a robot.

Dear Winston,

We're having our second baby seven years after the first – any tips on how we can do it better this time around?

Aarav, 41, Brighton

I am sure that the mistakes of that time will not be repeated; we should probably make another set of mistakes.

Dear Winston,

My son isn't trying hard in English. What do I say to him?

Archie, 44, Stockport

Men will forgive a man anything except bad prose.

Dear Winston,

My seven-year-old daughter has just found out that the tooth fairy isn't real and she's angry at her mother and me — she says we've lied to her! How should I respond?

Joshua, 42, Poole

Perhaps we have been guilty of some terminological inexactitudes.

Dear Winston,

When's an appropriate age to start giving my son chores?

Tom, 34, Peterborough

Youth is for freedom and reform, maturity for judicious compromise, and old age for stability and repose.

Dear Winston,

My daughter has developed a fear of dogs. How do I help her to be brave about it?

Michael, 35, Huddersfield

You will never get to the end of the journey if you stop to shy a stone at every dog that barks.

Dear Winston,

I want my son to stop eating his bogies.
What do I do?

Christopher, 38, Ipswich

It is always
more easy to
discover and
proclaim general
principles than to
apply them.

Dear Winston,

Potty training begins tomorrow! Any
words of wisdom for me and my partner?

Reyansh, 29, Telford

We
must be
united, we must
be undaunted,
we must be
inflexible.

Dear Winston,

My daughter keeps asking me what
happens when we die and I don't know
how to answer her. Help!

Oscar, 30, West Bromwich

Everyone
will have equal
rights in Heaven.
That will be the
real Welfare
State.

Dear Winston,

We've decided to take away the dummy
this weekend. Give us some advice?

David, 28, London

I am an
optimist. It does
not seem too much
use being anything
else.

Dear Winston,

My daughter's getting sassier and sassier –
we've introduced a time-out but it's so
tricky to maintain. Help!

Daniel, 33, Birmingham

Never give in,
never give in, never,
never, never, never – in
nothing, great or small,
large or petty – never
give in except to
convictions of honour
and good sense.

Dear Winston,

We've just started our baby on solids and I'm about to change his first nappy since then. What pep talk can I give myself?

Wayne, 26, Chatham

Let us therefore brace ourselves to our duties, and so bear ourselves that if the British Empire and its Commonwealth last for a thousand years, men will still say: 'This was their finest hour.'

Dear Winston,

What should I read to my four-year-old?
Peppa Pig or the Faraway Tree?

James, 36, Liverpool

There is a rule that before getting a new book, one should read an old classic. (Yet, as an author, I should not recommend too strict an adherence to this rule.)

Dear Winston,

I have to teach my son about the birds
and the bees. Any advice?

Alfred, 36, Preston

It's an
extraordinary
business, this way of
bringing babies into
the world. I don't
know how God
thought of it.

Dear Winston,

Why do babies cry?

Joseph, 33, Bristol

There are men in the world who derive as stern an exaltation from the proximity of disaster and ruin, as others from success.

Dear Winston,

My kids are such fussy eaters! I know I should be firm and make them eat their vegetables but I'm thinking it might be easier to just feed them fish fingers until they're 16. What do you think?

Andrew, 39, Sheffield

Victory at all costs, victory in spite of all terror, victory however long and hard the road may be; for without victory there is no survival!

Dear Winston,

How do kids get nits?

Robert, 31, Leeds

Virtuous motives,
trammelled by inertia
and timidity, are no
match for armed and
resolute wickedness.

Dear Winston,

What's your position on co-sleeping?

Ryan, 30, Manchester

Never
stand so high
upon a principle
that you cannot lower
it to suit the
circumstances.

Dear Winston,

My baby won't sleep unless my wife is
holding him, but we really want to get
him to sleep in the cot. Any tips?

Brandon, 36, Coventry

If he
sleeps he
must not be
wantonly
disturbed.

Dear Winston,

My son is begging to know what he's
getting for his birthday so much I think I
might tell him. What do you think?

Leo, 43, Northampton

I always avoid
prophesying
beforehand, because it
is much better policy to
prophesy after the
event has already
taken place.

Dear Winston,

My little girl has just got her first gold
star at school. What should I say to her?

Justin, 29, Leicester

The price of
greatness is
responsibility.

Dear Winston,

My wife and I went on an anniversary
holiday for a week and left our children
with my parents. During that time my
eldest son broke his leg when my eldest
daughter pushed him off the trampoline,
my youngest son bit a boy at nursery and
my youngest daughter ran away in the
shopping centre, causing my mum to
have a panic attack. What do I write in
their thank-you card?

William, 42, Bradford

Never
in the field
of human conflict
was so much owed
by so many to
so few.

Dear Winston,

My son has spent the last few months being as naughty as anything. I want to get better at discipline because I can't deal with the phone calls from his teacher any more – it's so embarrassing. Give me a pep talk?

Jonathan, 35, Nottingham

Do not let us speak of darker days; let us speak rather of sterner days. These are not dark days: these are great days – the greatest days our country has ever lived.

Dear Winston,

When I was at school there were nine
planets in the solar system. My eight-
year-old son came home from school
today and told me there were eight. I told
him he was wrong and thought it was the
hill I would die on. It turns out things
have changed – I missed the news about
Pluto – and he's correct. Make me feel
better?

Jason, 36, Stoke-on-Trent

The greatest
lesson in life is
to know that even
fools are right
sometimes.

Dear Winston,

My daughter is frightened of her first day at school. What can I say to her?

Aryan, 32, Hull

Courage is rightly esteemed the first of human qualities ... because it is the quality that guarantees all others.

Dear Winston,

My two kids won't stop bickering. What can I say to break up their fighting?

Elijah, 44, Portsmouth

> If the human race wishes to have a prolonged and indefinite period of material prosperity, they have only got to behave in a peaceful and helpful way towards one another.

Dear Winston,

My toddler keeps biting me. How do I
make it stop?

Aleksander, 29, Wolverhampton

Sure I am of
this, that you have
only to endure to
conquer.

REGARDING
TEENAGE
CHILDREN

Dear Winston,

My son keeps pestering me to let him have his first drink (he's 16). Should I let him? What should I give him?

Jeremy, 40, Ecclesfield

A single glass of champagne imparts a feeling of exhilaration. The nerves are braced, the imagination is agreeably stirred, the wits become more nimble. A bottle produces the contrary effect.

Dear Winston,

I'm helping my son with an English essay
but I was always rubbish at it at school.
What advice can I give him?

Richard, 39, Bembridge

Short words are
best and the old
words when short are
best of all.

Dear Winston,

My daughter's fallen in with a group of
bullies, but she's not a nasty girl herself.
What's going on?

Benjamin, 45, Tiptree

An appeaser is
one who feeds a
crocodile — hoping
that it will eat
him last.

Dear Winston,

My son sleeps in so much at the weekend – he keeps telling me he'll get up before 12 but he never follows through. What should I say to him?

William, 38, Plymouth

I thought he was a young man of promise; but it appears he is a young man of promises.

Dear Winston,

My daughter is addicted to Instagram and I'm sure it's making her unhappy. What do I do?

Kevin, 44, Derby

It would be a great reform in politics if wisdom could be made to spread as easily and as rapidly as folly.

Dear Winston,

Now my son is 18 he keeps saying he's an adult and that he can do what he likes, and I'm finding it hard to swallow. Any advice?

Eric, 50, Southampton

It has been said that democracy is the worst form of government except all those other forms that have been tried from time to time.

Dear Winston,

I really don't like my daughter's teacher and feel like he's picking on her. What do you think?

Kyle, 47, Bradfield

We know that he has, more than any other man, the gift of compressing the largest amount of words into the smallest amount of thought.

Dear Winston,

I'm 99% sure my son (15) has started smoking, and that he keeps lying to me about it. What can I say to him?

Adam, 45, Cranleigh

> The only guide to a man is his conscience; the only shield to his memory is the rectitude and sincerity of his actions.

Dear Winston,

My daughter's boyfriend has just broken up with her and I want to say something that will cheer her up. Any ideas?

Alan, 47, Nether Wallop

He looks like a female llama who has just been surprised in her bath.

Dear Winston,

My 19-year-old daughter got home at 3 a.m. drunk as a skunk. Should I be mad?

Thomas, 52, Kidlington

I have been brought up and trained to have the utmost contempt for people who get drunk.

Dear Winston,

My daughter is 13 and wants to be a
vegetarian. I wouldn't mind except I do
all the cooking and vegetarian food isn't
in my repertoire. What are your thoughts
on the subject?

Jeffrey, 53, Rustington

I am glad I
am not a
herbivore.

Dear Winston,

My son is taking a beating (verbally) from his history teacher. He's usually very clever, so he's not dealing with it very well. But constructive criticism is a good thing, right?

Stephen, 50, Belton

I do not resent criticism, even when, for the sake of emphasis, it parts for the time with reality.

Dear Winston,

My daughter has asked me what I think
of her new boyfriend. He's an all right
lad, bit wet and stupid, but she's 14 so in
any case I hate him on principle. What
do I say?

Aaron, 50, Meopham

He has many good
qualities, some of
which lie hidden, and he
has many bad qualities,
all of which are in the
shop window.

Dear Winston,

My son's first play opened this week and the reviews aren't great. What do I say to him to make him feel better?

Sean, 47, Cairncross

It is better to be making the news than taking it; to be an actor rather than a critic.

Dear Winston,

It's New Year's Day and my kids are old enough now to work out that I'm not poorly – I've actually got a stonking hangover. Do I acknowledge it? What do I say?

Mark, 57, Beaconsfield

All I can say is that I have taken more out of alcohol than alcohol has taken out of me.

Dear Winston,

My daughter's going off travelling for her gap year. Any advice?

Rahul, 55, Didling

When you are leaving for an unknown destination, it is a good plan to attach a restaurant car at the tail of the train.

Dear Winston,

My son admitted to me that his girlfriend stayed over last night without my knowledge, and that she escaped out of his bedroom window down the drainpipe. I'm finding it so impressive I'm not sure I can keep a straight face and dole out a punishment. What do you think?

Scott, 60, Canterbury

This is one of those cases in which the imagination is baffled by the facts.

Dear Winston,

My daughter won't stop asking me for
more money at the weekend. What can I
tell her to get her to back off?

Frank, 40, Cheshunt

I have nothing
to offer but
blood, toil, tears
and sweat.

Dear Winston,

My teenage son has ginger hair and some of the other kids at school are teasing him about it. What can I tell him to say back to them next time they start on him?

Ben, 36, Beverley

We will have no truce or parley with you, or the grisly gang who do your wicked will.

Dear Winston,

One of my girls keeps asking me for help
with her trigonometry homework but I
just can't do it. What should I say?

Jake, 48, Poole

It is a
riddle wrapped
in a mystery
in a mystery
inside an
enigma.

Dear Winston,

My son came home last night (a school night) very drunk. He says I can't tell him off because he was home before his curfew (10.30 p.m.) and I never said he couldn't drink. What do you think?

Patrick, 55, Caistor

Perhaps it is better to be irresponsible and right than to be responsible and wrong.

Dear Winston,

My son and I had a bet on who would win the Premier League – he won and won't shut up about it. What do I say to get him to put a lid on it?

Tyler, 48, Callow End

> A fanatic is one who can't change his mind and won't change the subject.

Dear Winston,

What do I say to my kids to teach them
about 'fake news'?

Dustin, 60, Calloose

There are a
terrible lot of
lies going around the
world, and the worst of
it is half of them
are true.

Dear Winston,

My son is doing a science degree.
I'm very proud, but he's getting a bit
smug about it and says science is more
important than the arts. What should I
say to him?

Nathan, 48, Camps End

> The latest
> refinements of
> science are linked
> with the cruelties of
> the Stone Age.

Dear Winston,

My son is spending a lot of his money on going out with his friends. I don't want to tell him what to do any more now he's at university, but I think he's being irresponsible. What do you think?

Abioye, 50, Canning Town

I have in my life concentrated more on self-expression than on self-denial.

Dear Winston,

My daughter's new boyfriend is very polite and clever but he's boring. How do I tell her this?

Samuel, 45, Kenton

Never trust a man who has not a single redeeming vice.

Dear Winston,

I let my 14-year-old son watch a film rated 18 with his friends. My wife received three complaints from the friends' parents so of course I pretended I didn't give them permission. She keeps talking to me about it and I'm rubbish at lying. What can I say to make it convincing when she mentions it again?

Gregory, 55, Keele

What kind of people do they think we are?

Dear Winston,

My son wants to know about my
university days but I prefer to keep those
secrets to myself. Should I own up to all
my vices or should I gloss over them?

Bryan, 47, Kegworth

Sometimes
truth is so
precious it must
be attended by a
bodyguard of
lies.

Dear Winston,

My daughter has her first GCSE
tomorrow — it's geography. Any advice?

Bradley, 55, Heyrod

If you have
an important
point to make, don't
try to be subtle or
clever. Use a pile driver.
Hit the point once. Then
come back and hit it again.
Then hit it a third
time — a tremendous
whack.

Dear Winston,

My son turns 18 today and I want to teach him how to be a responsible, upright and clean-cut young man. How can I do that?

Jesse, 60, Keith Inch

I must point out that my rule of life prescribes as an absolute sacred rite smoking cigars and also the drinking of alcohol before, after, and if need be during all meals and in the intervals between them.

Dear Winston,

I don't like my son's science teacher and want to give him a good dressing down at parents' evening. What should I say?

Jordan, 39, Henley-on-Thames

Dear Winston,

I'm taking my daughters paintballing today. Any tips?

Shaun, 45, Heywood

Nothing in life is so exhilarating as to be shot at without result.

Dear Winston,

My children talk in slang all the time.
How can I get them to speak proper
English?

Peter, 39, Weasdale

This is the
sort of English up
with which I will
not put.

Dear Winston,

How do I tell my son that it's better to talk things out than fight with your fists?

Juan, 50, Weedon

To jaw-jaw is always better than to war-war.

REGARDING GROWN-UP CHILDREN

Dear Winston,

My son and I disagree on politics but he insists on talking to me about it at the dinner table. What can I say to shut him up?

Ronald, 67, Sipson

Dull, Duller, Dulles.

Dear Winston,

My wife died 18 months ago and my daughter keeps trying to encourage me to do more social activities, but I'm not ready. What can I say to get her to back off?

Nathaniel, 58, Skeyton

I am certainly not one of those who need to be prodded. In fact, if anything, I am a prod.

Dear Winston,

My son's Irish wife is called Moira and he says it embarrasses him that I can't say her name correctly. Is he right?

Donald, 60, Rainworth

Everybody has a right to pronounce foreign names as he chooses.

Dear Winston,

My daughter says I never admit when I'm wrong. What should I say back to her?

Carlos, 54, Smythe's Green

Eating my words has never given me indigestion.

Dear Winston,

My son's late to everything and it drives
me mad. Am I right to hound him about
it or should I let it go?

Lewis, 48, Rait

Unpunctuality
is a vile habit,
and all my life
I have tried to
break myself
of it.

Dear Winston,

My son and his family are thinking of
moving to America and I don't want
them to. What can I tell him about the
US to put him off?

Craig, 55, Marlborough

Toilet paper
too thin,
newspapers
too fat.

Dear Winston,

My daughter is moving in with a man I
don't like – he's not going anywhere with
his life and he can't stand up for himself.
How do I explain this to her?

Stan, 60, Salford

He is a sheep
in sheep's
clothing.

Dear Winston,

My son's about to propose to his girlfriend. Any words of encouragement?

Derek, 50, Llanbradach

My most brilliant achievement was to persuade my wife to marry me.

Dear Winston,

My son is 34 and has quit his second
career. I feel it's time he settled on one
profession but now he thinks he might
go travelling! What's wrong with this
generation?

Vincent, 60, Cardiff

So they go on, in
strange paradox,
decided only to be
undecided, resolved to be
irresolute, adamant for
drift, solid for
fluidity, all-powerful
to be impotent.

Dear Winston,

My son wants me to invest in his new business of growing basil plants in test tubes. Should I do it?

Gabriel, 72, Belfast

He will bankrupt you before you start.

Dear Winston,

My daughter keeps asking me questions about what I got up to in my youth – it's sweet of her, but I'd rather not disclose what I was doing in the 70s. What should I say to her?

Drew, 66, Hadleigh

If the present tries to sit in judgement of the past, it will lose the future.

Dear Winston,

My son's husband is very good looking but he's so full of himself. I want to give my opinion to my son in a way that sounds clever so he doesn't get cross with me. Any suggestions?

Trevor, 56, Dundee

He is always patting himself on the back, a kind of exercise that contributes to his excellent physical condition.

Dear Winston,

My son is a teacher and keeps forcing
me to go into school and give talks to
his students about my job (I am a retired
tightrope walker). What can I say to get
him to leave me alone?

Seth, 68, Hull

I refuse to be
exhibited like a
prize bull whose chief
attraction is his
past prowess.

Dear Winston,

My daughter is a nervous traveller and insists on us getting to the airport three hours before our departure time. She's being ridiculous, isn't she?

Adrian, 52, Derry

I am a sporting man. I always like to give aeroplanes a fair chance of getting away.

Dear Winston,

I'm an organised man so I'm planning
my funeral so that my children don't
need to worry, but I'm struggling with
an epitaph to go on my gravestone. Any
recommendations?

Larry, 70, Mudford Sock

I am ready to
meet my Maker.
Whether my Maker is
ready for the ordeal
of meeting me is
another matter.

Dear Winston,

My son and daughter-in-law are hosting
Christmas lunch this year; they have
funny traditions and I know I'm going to
be roped into some novelty board game.
How do I communicate the right way of
doing things?

Mario, 66, Eckington

My idea of a good
dinner is, first to
have good food, then
discuss good food, and
after this good food has
been elaborately discussed,
to discuss a good topic —
with me as chief
conversationalist.

Dear Winston,

My daughter says I'm getting arrogant in my old age, but I think I'm just honest. You're an egoist too, right?

Luke, 74, Inverness

Of course I'm an egoist. Where do you get if you aren't?

Dear Winston,

My son says I'm being too hard on him about his dream to become a musician, but it's such a tricky industry to break into, and in all honesty I don't think he has what it takes. What do you think?

Jerry, 53, Edworth

Diplomacy is the art of telling plain truths without giving offence.

Dear Winston,

My daughter has her first job interview tomorrow. Any last-minute tips?

Roger, 50, Hitchin

Attitude is a little thing that makes a big difference.

Dear Winston,

I'm winning at Risk against my 50-year-old son for the first time in 30 years! Give me something pithy to throw at him.

Gary, 76, Edinburgh

> In the depths of that dusty soul there is nothing but abject surrender.

Dear Winston,

My daughter and her husband are
thinking of moving to Canada as they
think it will be a better life for the kids,
but selfishly I want them nearby to take
care of me in my old age. How do I tell
them that?

Allen, 57, Cromford

Do not let
plans for a new
world divert your
energies from saving
what is left of
the old.

Dear Winston,

My daughter's throwing me a 70th birthday party and she's going overboard. What should I say to her to calm it down (bearing in mind I still want a fun party!)?

Lucas, 69, Gairloch

I am easily satisfied with the best.

Dear Winston,

My wife keeps describing my daughter's new boyfriend as the 'strong, silent type' and it's starting to annoy me. What's so good about being strong and silent?

Johnny, 49, Ganllwyd

Too often the strong silent man is silent because he does not know what to say, and is reputed strong only because he has remained silent.

Dear Winston,

My son today becomes a history teacher and I'm very proud. What should I write in his card?

Danny, 62, Haine

A nation that forgets its past has no future.

Dear Winston,

My daughter's worrying so much about the future. What can I say to help her relax about it all?

Lawrence, 47, Truro

It is always wise to look ahead, but difficult to look farther than you can see.

Dear Winston,

Last week my son and I had the worst
argument we've ever had. How do I
apologise?

Dylan, 68, Newquay

The worst
quarrels only
arise when both sides
are equally in the
right and in the
wrong.

Dear Winston,

My daughter's going out with a two-faced, nasty little man. She's forcing us to have a dinner and says I have to be civil. What can I say to explain to her that I'll do it for her sake but it will be all show?

Bobby, 58, Hadden

I'll kiss him on both cheeks — or, if you prefer, on all four.

Dear Winston,

My daughter's trying to get me into golf
because she says it will keep me active.
How do I tell her that I find it very
boring?

Francis, 69, Cambridge

Golf is a game
whose aim is to hit
a very small ball into
an even smaller hole, with
weapons singularly ill
designed for the
purpose.

Dear Winston,

My daughter is thinking about quitting her job and setting up a café. She doesn't have any skills in that area and her chances of getting a business loan are slim. Should I point all this out to her, or be supportive?

Colin, 60, Stevenage

Don't argue about the difficulties. The difficulties will argue for themselves.

Dear Winston,

My son is getting into tarot and I think it's a load of baloney. How do I say that to him?

Wayne, 57, Bradford

Tell me more about that trollop.

Dear Winston,

My daughter and I couldn't agree the other day on how you pronounce the word *Schadenfreude*. Annoyingly, I heard someone say it her way on the telly just now. Should I admit it to her?

Paul, 69, Wigan

It is a fine thing to be honest, but it is also very important to be right.

Dear Winston,

What should I write in my son's 40th birthday card?

Roy, 68, Ripon

Now this is not the end. It is not even the beginning of the end. But it is, perhaps, the end of the beginning.

10 THINGS YOU MIGHT NOT KNOW ABOUT WINSTON CHURCHILL

1. He won the Nobel Prize in Literature in 1953.

2. He was granted honorary American citizenship and was half American through his mother.

3. He switched between political parties, being first a Conservative, then a Liberal, and then going back to the Conservatives.

4. As a war correspondent in South Africa in 1899, he was captured and put in a prison camp – which he escaped from by scaling a wall under the cover of darkness.

5. His record isn't blemish-free: evidence suggests he held racist views, and

questionable events he was responsible for or contributed to include Gallipoli in 1915 (where the Allies sustained 250,000 casualties) and the 1943 famine in India in which three million people died.

6. He was a descendant of William the Conqueror, who was his 24th great-grandfather.

7. He is the only prime minister to have made it onto the music charts: first in 1965, shortly after his death, via a collection of his speeches, and again on an album titled *Reach for the Skies* released to mark the 70th anniversary of the Battle of Britain.

8. He took 60 bottles of alcohol with him on his journey to the Boer War.

9. He painted over 500 works, and 50 of them were displayed at the Royal Academy, the first of them in 1947, submitted under the pseudonym David Winter.

10. He was a keen bricklayer.

If you liked this book,
You might also like ...

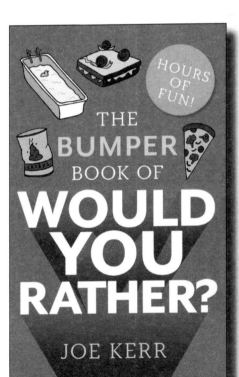

HOURS OF FUN!

THE
BUMPER
BOOK OF
WOULD
YOU
RATHER?

JOE KERR

Dear Winston,

My son bought me this book as a gift and it's all right, but I must say I was hoping for a gift voucher instead.

Fred, 62, North Piddle

It is a good thing for an uneducated man to read books of quotations.